Contents

Forward	
Light	The beginning
Know the Light	Peace is Knowing the Light
Capture the Light	Cannot capture, you must enter
Song of Light	New love that dies
Twisted Light	Beginning of lies deceit
Shadowed Light	A slave to untruth
Soul Cry	Escape the black empty abyss of self
Spirit of Light	Always there
Light of Ruth	A friend shares light
Red Rose Given	The light of love given
Essence of Light	Knowing the calm
Light of Truth	Conquers all
Light of You	Spiritual partner – souls becoming one

The verse written was inspired by life and the people in it. "Light of You" is inspired by my wife, Michelle, and our journey to becoming spiritual partners. We all battle hurt, lost, and times of total despair, yet the most constant and fierce battle, for me, is the battle of self. I have found that the battle of self is eased when we enter fully into the light of truth and embrace it. Do this and you will experience the rewards of peace and calm, joy, love, and the contentment of knowing who you are and why you exist. My hope is that the verse and images in this small book help you on your journey of life.

FORWARD

By exploring the subject of light through verse and image I have attempted to capture the drama of human experience. Each of us throughout our lives experience the joy of acceptance and love; the pain of rejection and indifference; the confusion of fear and hate; the discovery of true love; the crushing blow of lost love; the dark hole of self-pity and lost hope; the false path of pride; and finally, hopefully, the peace, humility and contentment of knowing who we are and why we exist, when we stand fully in the Light.

ACKNOWLEGDEMENTS

FORWARD	Photo By: J R Lowe – Light Dance
LIGHT	Photo By: S K Findsen
KNOW THE LIGHT	Photo By: S K Findsen
CAPTURE THE LIGHT	Photo By: Kathryn Findsen
SONG OF LIGHT	Photo By: J R Lowe
TWISTED LIGHT	Photo By: S K Findsen
SHADOWED LIGHT	Photo By: J R Lowe
SOUL CRY	Photo By: S K Findsen
SPIRIT OF LIGHT	Photo By: S K Findsen
LIGHT OF RUTH	Photo By: J R Lowe
RED ROSE GIVEN	Photo By: J R Lowe
ESSENCE OF LIGHT	Photo By: J R Lowe
LIGHT OF TRUTH	Photo By: J R Lowe
THE LIGHT OF YOU	Photo By: Kathryn Findsen

Light

We are conceived in light

We are known through light

We are eagles soaring on light

We are sustained by light

With light, we obtain knowledge

Light, the essence of all that is good

Light, the finality of all that is true

Light, the completeness of happiness

Light, the overflowing of Red Rose Given

With light, we clearly see

With light, we delight in truth

With light, we achieve the grace of sharing

Seek, discover, embrace, and become light

Revealing, with pure light, the soul

S. K. Findsen

Know the Light

Search, discover with honest sincere soul

An unshackled spirit a boon will be

Wing to Light, drive darkness behind

Humble the spirit, Greet the Light

Light and time are common friends

From all time before and all time future

With patience approach from eager heart

Gentle quiet hunger, Embrace the Light

Greet true light, greet true nature

Shadow and darkness will cease

Lighting up mind, heart and soul

Only the honest and brave, Enter the Light

O' courageous, O' brave heart, O' seeker of truth

O' humble soul, O' alpha of wisdom, Know the Light

S. K. Findsen

Capture the Light

Run, run light chaser, capture the light

Sure and shift your movements must be

Grasp it, hold it with strength and might

Open the hand and the light will flee

Stealth is the answer, the light shall be mine

Control it, hide it, barter it, O' fortune great

Only for me shall the prized light shine

Mold it, possess it, on me the light will wait

Black the night, lost is the light treasured

Sight gone, the light is no more, blind am I

Confused, hope gone, terror not measured

Darkness close, suffocating, I wish, fear to die

O' wait, a glimmer, light of hope devours the night!

Shinning day speaks. Hark, enter the light

S. K. Findsen

Song of Light

Crisp sparkles of morning light

Dance and swirl into your mind

Destroying darkness of leaping soul

Seeking birth of a Song of Light

Heart rhythms soar and stain

Breaking free in whiteness found

Yet still bright blindness grows

Yearns the breath for a Song of Light

Shadows grow oh crimson heart

Heave and flail with echoes strong

Dagger cuts soul's coming gloom

Consumes devours the Song of Light

Weeping mind and sorrow wails

Night folds on Song of Light

S. K. Findsen

Twisted Light

Daggered heart, weeping spirit, empty soul

The brilliant road of true light pains the sight

Light twisted in Darkness is an easier path

Sooth spirit, fill soul and heart with Twisted light

Empty agony shrouded in darkness deep

Times of numbness ease painful heart

For a blessed moment comfort is found

In the brief solace of Twisted Light

Rise again O' Daggered heart and empty soul

Come again O' Clouded mind, O' weeping spirit

Greater darkness, diminished light to cover the pain

Common venomous orb of Twisted light

Slowly night descends, tightening the grip of Twisted Light

Screaming empty soul, daggered heart; listen, the Soul Cries

S. K. Findsen

Shadowed Light

Toy, flirt, dance on the edge of total night

Light one, Darkness another; crossroad of Twisted Light

Shadowed Light allures, it beckons, come, explore

Sprinting heart, yearning soul, discover Shadowed Light

Dark spirit of pain comes; covered by Shadowed Light

Void empty soul cries out; filled with Shadowed Light

Whirling winds comes to mind; follow Shadowed Light

The true light waxes faint, distant; in Shadowed Light

Full circle, last view taken, true light not seen

Slight cold breeze pushes forth into night

The soul shivers within, testament of fear unknown

Pulse roars, pounds, rushes, in the blind empty night

Pulse covers the agony, fills the void, focuses the night wind

Empty pulse wanes in the darkness, beyond Shadowed Light

S. K. Findsen

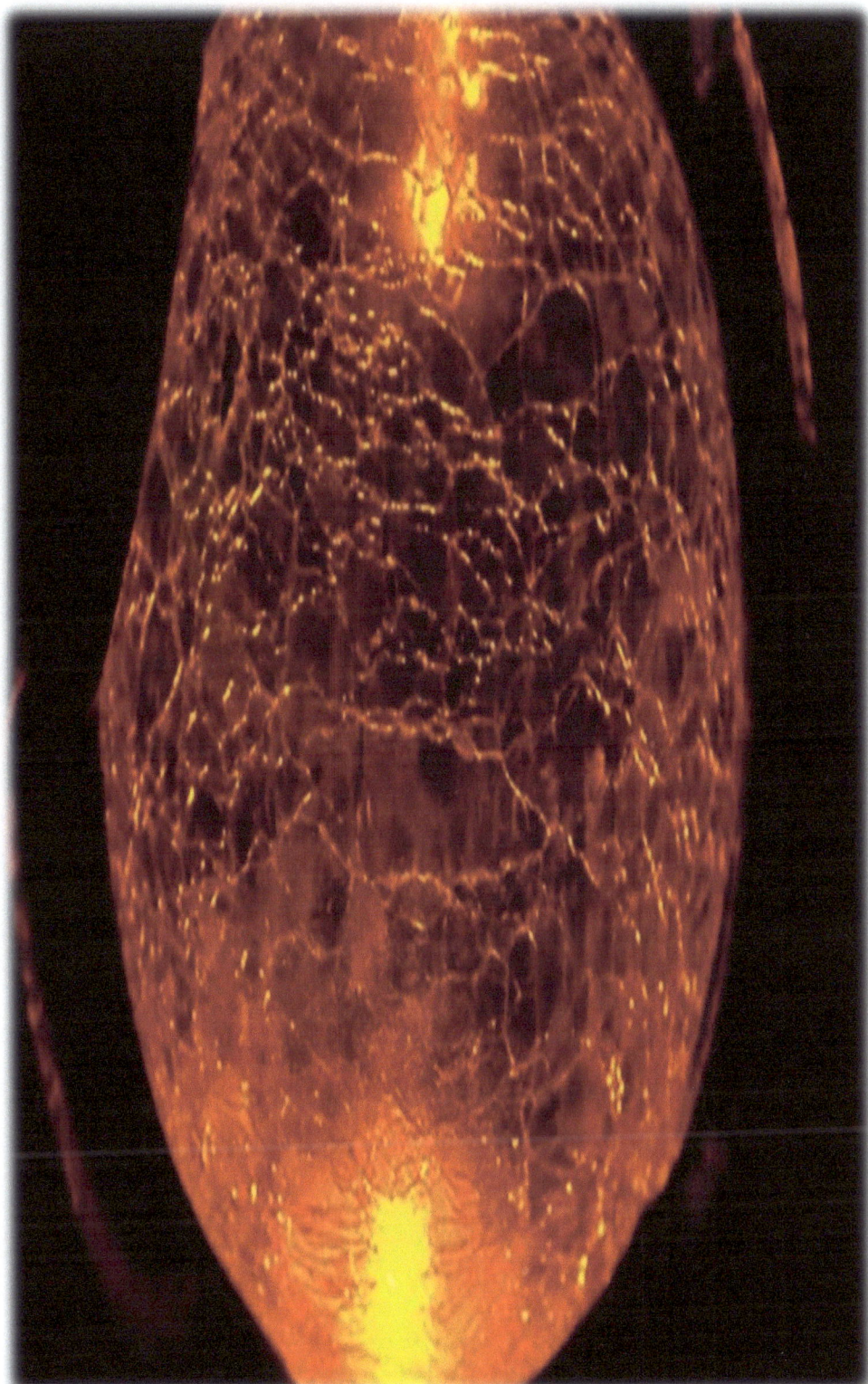

Soul Cry

New Light shines, a rainbow bright of freedom's arcing joy
Times and time gush with expectancy of hope and shine
Sweet laughing waters lift New Light into soul's freedom pass
O, the mystery of undiscovered light and broken light, lies here

Beard and sands echo black, New Light a silent screaming soul
The beard is known yet not known with soul's freedom lost
Dark anguish shrouds New Light on edge of whirling winds
O to find the mystery to mend the light and free the soul

Echoes strong, echoes weak, New Light's soul cry echoes roll
Within the empty pit of night, New light seeks to echo, to soar
Echoes trapped gathered, True Light extends a mending glow
Free from soul cry and whirling winds, New Light shines within

Soul cry rallies beards and sands to battle back the night
Hammering back whirling winds with freedom of the soul

S. K. Findsen

Spirit of Light

Through desperate continuous echoes

My mind screamed silently for something anything

To control, to comfort, to placate, to quench

The empty chaotic darkness, burning within my soul

O' black sleep would have been welcome

To quiet the agony of nothingness

To put to rest the unworthiness, shame of me

Falling, falling into the empty abyss of self

Engulfed in darkness, in the pit of blackness

Turned away the Spirit of Light time and times

My dark soul would not let me choose

Yet, the Spirit of Light was always there

Gently there, offering the gift of light, peace, knowing

Choose the light, choose the light, I chose

S. K. Findsen

Light of Ruth

O' gentle Ruth, O' fairest lady

Your garden of lights beam forth

With simple joy and healing hope

Sharing precious light with sadden soul

Flowing liqueur from Light of Ruth

Heals dimmed light of wounded spirit

Striking forth bright, a shining day

Giving solace to daggered heart

Sustain the beams of healing light

The soaring light, of Red Rose Given

Raise and wing with light of color

O' mended heart, O' peaceful soul

To Light of Ruth, O' colored orb

Comes the fullness of thankful heart

S. K. Findsen

Red Rose Given

The morning light shines in darkness red

Exposing natural rose of shadowed heart

The click of time is new revealed

Lumens the heart with, Red Rose Given

Receive the moving light with all repose

Decline not the solitary echo of shine

Heed the gift of darkened light offered

Share without constraint, Red Rose Given

Escape shadows of ancient light

Spread wing and soar the tested wind

Cut shadowed heart for freedoms sake

Release the swirling, Red Rose Given

O' if all sands and beards embraced

The soaring light, of Red Rose Given

S. K. Findsen

Essence of Light

Calm warmth of clear day, Light surrounds you

Shields you from all that may harm

Seal your sight, unwrap your soul, free your mind

Release time, and trust, the Essence of Light

Let your mind float in the light of pure day

Inhale the sweet joy of essence given

Fear not, want not, free from all storms

Give yourself wholly to the Essence of light

You touch it, you hear it, you desire it

The calm, the stillness in your soul, your heart

The peacefulness of your slumber will come

You will see clearly, from the Essence of Light

Share the treasure, reveal the gold, impart the joy

Red Rose Given is Essence of Light

S. K. Findsen

LIGHT OF TRUTH

Buried in the dark souls of beards

Full grown foliage feeds darkest hour

Thorns shroud dark truth's hollow light

The Light of Truth pulses and breaths

The eyes of beards with fullness see

Only the twisting swirling light deceives

Time and times must lowly bow

To Light of Truth, the force of day

O' brightest light, O' purest form remains

Wind nor magic, or Red beard's twisted light

No power of the skies, or soil below

Shall hold confine the ageless Light of Truth

All songs are sung, all souls revealed

Light of Truth, conquers, triumphs over all

S. K. Findsen

The Light of You

Here I am, it's quiet early in the morning

All the work is done, sleepy, thinking of you

Thinking of your warm soft body next to mine

Touching feeling holding, brushing my lips

On your smooth skin

The Light of you

Sharing thoughts, a laugh, a soft touch

Searching deep in our eyes to know us better

The Light of you

Holding your hand as we walk

On a crisp morning of life, sharing us

Whispering about everything and nothing

The Light of you

Looking into the starry night

Searching exploring the sky finding that

Special Light, yours and mine, ours

The Light of you

Holding tight snug warm, falling in

Love, falling asleep holding us

Dreaming of you

S. K. Findsen